W9-AAZ-783

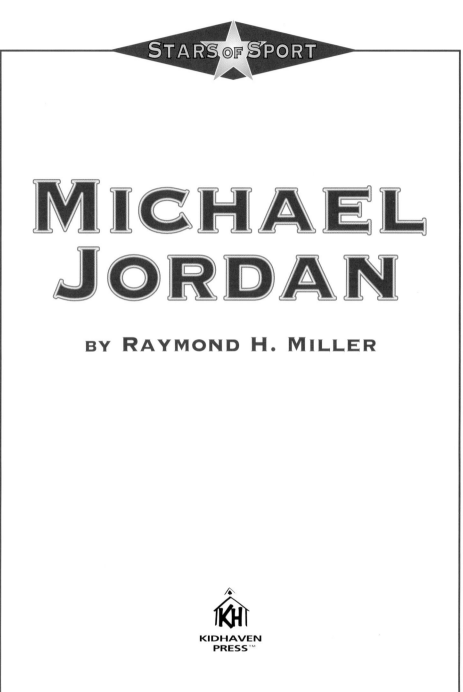

STARS OF SPORT

MICHAEL JORDAN

BY RAYMOND H. MILLER

KIDHAVEN PRESS™

THOMSON

———— ✦ ————™

GALE

San Diego • Detroit • New York • San Francisco • Cleveland
New Haven, Conn. • Waterville, Maine • London • Munich

THOMSON

GALE

Picture Credits

Cover Photo: Associated Press, AP
© AFP/CORBIS, 34
Associated Press, AP, 12, 18, 24, 25, 36
Associated Press, Chicago Sun-Times, 26
© Bettmann/CORBIS, 19, 21
© Duomo/CORBIS, 7, 9, 13, 39
© Wally McNamee/CORBIS, 5, 15
Brandy Noon, 17, 28, 31
Photos12.com, 35
© Reuters NewMedia, Inc./CORBIS 10, 40, 41

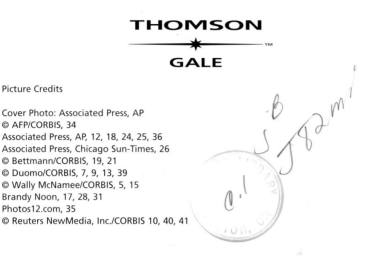

For more information, contact
KidHaven Press
27500 Drake Rd.
Farmington Hills, MI 48331-3535
Or you can visit our Internet site at http://www.gale.com

LIBRARY OF CONGRESS CATALOGING-IN-PUBLICATION DATA

Miller, Raymond H., 1967–
  Michael Jordan / by Raymond H. Miller
    p. cm.—(Stars of sport.)
  Summary: Examines the life and career of the high-scoring Chicago Bulls player,
who made a brief attempt to play minor league baseball in 1994 and returned to
play basketball with the Washington Wizards in 2001.
  Includes bibliographical references and index.
  ISBN 0-7377-1421-2 (hard : alk. paper)
  1. Jordan, Michael, 1963– . Juvenile literature. 2. Basketball players—United
States—Biography—Juvenile literature. [1. Jordan, Michael, 1963— 2. Basketball
players. 3. African Americans—Biography.] I. Title. II. Series.
  GV884 .J67 M55 2003
  796.323'092—dc21

                                                    2002007173

Printed in the United States of America

Contents

Heart of a Champion

Michael Jordan was already famous when he joined the Chicago Bulls in 1984. He was a two-time, first-team **All-American** guard at the University of North Carolina, and he scored the winning basket in the 1982 National Collegiate Athletic Association (NCAA) championship game as a freshman.

Playing in the National Basketball Association (NBA), he quickly became the game's premier scorer and earned the nickname "Air Jordan" for his high-flying slam dunks. Though Jordan had a reputation for being the best player in the world, the Bulls lost in the playoffs the first six years of his career. Then, playing for a new coach in the early 1990s, Jordan elevated his game and led the Bulls to three straight NBA titles. After a

Michael Jordan, in white, shoots over Georgetown Hoyas center Patrick Ewing in the 1982 NCAA championship game.

brief retirement he returned to win three more championships with Chicago.

Not everything has gone smoothly for Jordan. He has overcome controversy and personal tragedy. But he overcame both obstacles to become one of the greatest champions in the history of professional sports.

CHAPTER ONE

Late Bloomer

Michael Jeffrey Jordan was born on February 17, 1963, in Brooklyn, New York, to James and Deloris Jordan. He was the fourth of their five children, joining James Ronald, Larry, and Deloris. His sister Roslyn was born later. Shortly after Michael's birth the family moved to North Carolina, where they eventually settled near Wilmington.

James and Deloris taught their children the importance of staying out of trouble, though Michael did not always listen. When he was a young boy he picked up some frayed extension cords from the wet grass and was nearly electrocuted. Michael made a full recovery, but he continued to find trouble. Several years later, while chopping wood without shoes, he nearly cut off his big toe with the ax. His frequent brushes with danger did little to change his careless ways.

Michael was not only accident prone, he was also lazy. One summer the Jordan boys worked part-time in the fields cutting tobacco leaves. Michael hated the job, so on the second day he pretended to have a sore back. His brothers were not surprised when he did not have to go

Jordan's short haircut inspired his classmates to name him "bald head" when he was in elementary school.

back. When it came to doing chores around the house, Michael did not fake injury. He cleverly paid his brothers and sisters with his allowance to do his chores for him.

"Bald Head"

Michael was only lazy when it came to work. He spent a lot of time riding his bike and going to the ocean, which was located just a few miles away. But most of all, he played baseball. As a pitcher on his Little League team, he struck out opposing batters with a blazing fastball and led his team to the Little League state championship. His team won the game and he was named Most Valuable Player (MVP).

Michael was a star on the baseball field, but in school he was just the opposite. His classmates teased him and called him "bald head" because his hair was so short. He also had ears that stuck out.

When Michael was in high school the teasing stopped, and he began to fit in with the other kids. He was a good student, but playing sports was the main point of his life. He was a quarterback on the football team until he was injured and stopped playing. In baseball he was still a great pitcher. He even competed in the long jump on the track team. But basketball soon became his favorite, even though he was shorter than most boys his age. He often hung from a chin-up bar to try to stretch his body, but he remained well under six feet tall.

Backyard Rivalry

Michael's father saw how much his son loved basketball, so he built a court in the backyard. Michael and Larry

Michael, in a Chicago White Sox uniform, runs the bases during a major league exhibition game.

played one-on-one and developed a fierce rivalry. Larry had better basketball moves and could jump higher than Michael, so he often beat his younger brother. Michael hated finishing second at anything, so losing to Larry made him even more determined to become a better player. He practiced his dribbling and shooting daily and spent hours copying Larry's flashy moves.

9

Jordan shows his frustration and disappointment at losing a basketball game with the Washington Wizards.

Michael attended a summer basketball camp between his freshman and sophomore years and played well. He decided to try out for his high school varsity team the next season. When the tryouts ended the coach posted the varsity roster at the gymnasium, but Michael's name was not on it. He was crushed. When he got home he closed his bedroom door and cried the rest of the night.

Michael was determined to prove the coach had made a mistake. Every morning before school he practiced in the high school gym and began to improve rapidly. He played junior varsity (JV) that year and was known for his powerful slam dunks. With Michael on the team the JV games became popular. The varsity players got to the gym early just to see him play. After averaging twenty-five points a game, everyone could see Michael was going to be a star.

Growth Spurt

Standing only five feet ten inches tall, Michael knew he needed to grow to become a better player. But no one in his family was over six feet tall, and he was convinced he would remain short. Then, around the age of fifteen, he hit a growth spurt that put him well over six feet.

Michael took full advantage of his new height. He matched up well against tall players, yet he was still quick enough to take on shorter players. When he tried out for varsity again as a junior, he made the team with ease. Michael chose to wear number twenty-three—it was as close as he could get to half of forty-five, his brother Larry's number. Michael and Larry both were starting guards and they played well together, but the team finished just 13-10 that season.

As a senior, Michael was the star of the team. He used his incredible quickness to dribble past defenders. And when he jumped, he seemed to stay **airborne** longer than the other players. He averaged more than twenty points a game that season and nearly led his team to the state championship. But because Michael blossomed as a basketball star relatively late in high school, he did not make the national list of the top three hundred high school senior players. As a result, when it came time to select a college, he had few choices. He wanted to play at UCLA, his favorite team, but they did not offer him a scholarship. So he turned, instead, to one of the colleges in his home state that had recruited him: the University

"Air Jordan" performing one of his trademark slam dunks with the Chicago Bulls.

Michael Jordan at the free throw line as a North Carolina Tar Heel guard.

of North Carolina. After visiting the campus and talking to the team's head coach, Dean Smith, Michael fell in love with the school. A short while later Smith offered him a basketball scholarship. He accepted it and became a North Carolina Tar Heel.

Chapter Two

A Rising Star

Michael did not choose North Carolina solely for its successful basketball program. He was also drawn to its strong academic tradition. Despite playing several sports, he had been a good student in high school. It was important to his parents and Michael that he got a solid college education for life after basketball. He majored in geography at North Carolina and received good grades.

On the basketball court he impressed everyone with his shooting and jumping abilities. Few freshmen had ever played in the starting lineup at North Carolina under Dean Smith, but Michael was different. He was more mature than most freshmen, so Smith started him at the guard position. The team already had two future professional players, so Michael was not the star. But as the season went along, the team turned to him for an important jump shot or an exciting dunk to pump up the crowd. He finished the regular season as the Tar Heels' third leading scorer and was named Atlantic Coast Conference (ACC) Freshman of the Year.

Jordan going hard to the hoop against the Georgetown Hoyas in the 1982 NCAA championship game.

North Carolina made the 1982 NCAA Tournament and advanced to the championship game, where they met the Georgetown Hoyas. Michael scored just four points in the first half, but his hot shooting in the second half kept the Tar Heels in the game. Georgetown held a 62-61 lead with seconds remaining when Michael scored the winning basket. The clutch shot did more than thrust him into the national spotlight. "[The shot] awakened a person inside of me . . . to be one of the best, or be the best," he said. "That drove me, and I guess with that shot, it kind of ignited a fire inside of me that nothing was going to stop me."[1]

Michael did not let his sudden fame affect him. He continued practicing nearly every day that summer, and when the 1982–1983 season started, he was a much better player. He increased his scoring average to 19.7 points as a sophomore and was named first-team All-American. He also received the NCAA College Player of the Year award. Michael started slowly his junior year but came on strong later in the season to nearly match his scoring average from the year before. Again he was named first-team All-American and College Player of the Year.

Gold Medal Performance

After Michael's junior year he and Coach Smith decided he was ready to play in the NBA. In the 1984 NBA draft the Chicago Bulls selected Jordan in the first round. But before he moved to Chicago to start his pro career, he gained a spot on the 1984 U.S. Olympic basketball team. To prepare for the Olympics Jordan and his teammates played against a team of NBA stars, including "Magic" Johnson of the Los Angeles Lakers. Jordan earned praise for his fancy moves and amazing dunks. After one of the games Johnson told reporters that Jordan was easily the best player on the Olympic team.

Once the Olympic games started Jordan continued to receive rave reviews. After an easy win over Spain, the opposing coach called him a "rubber man" for the way he twisted his body in midair to avoid defenders. The U.S. team went on to win the gold medal as Jordan averaged seventeen points to lead the team. The U.S. coach, legendary Bobby Knight, called him the greatest player he had ever seen.

Jordan's University of North Carolina Basketball Statistics

Year	Games	Field Goal %	Free Throw %	Reb	Ast	Steals	Points
81–82	34	53.4	72.2	149	61	41	460
82–83	36	53.5	73.7	197	55	78	721
83–84	31	55.1	77.9	163	64	50	607

Michael Jordan's UNC Facts	
1982	NCAA Division I Championship
1983–1984	First Team All-American
1983–1984	*Sporting News* Player of the Year
1984	Wooden Award winner
1984	Naismith Award winner

Source: www.UNC.edu

Jordan sails by his opponents on a drive to the basket in the first game of the 1984 Olympics in Los Angeles.

Unbelieva-Bull Rookie

The Chicago Bulls were known as a losing team when Jordan reported to training camp after the Olympics in 1984. They had been to the play-offs only twice in the past nine years, and none the last three. But Jordan had grown accustomed to winning at North Carolina, so his goal was to lead the Bulls to the play-offs every year.

Jordan also wanted to make a good impression on his new coaches and teammates. Early in training camp, during a five-on-five scrimmage, his team jumped out to a 7-2 lead. The coach stopped the game and made Jordan switch teams, because he wanted to test the rookie. Playing with controlled anger, Jordan grabbed nearly every rebound and hit seven straight shots to lead his team to an 11-8 victory. It was an early indication of how much he wanted to win.

In his third game as a pro he scored thirty-seven points against the Milwaukee Bucks. He continued to play well the rest of the season and was typically the Bulls' leading scorer. But he did more than just put points on the board. He was also an accurate passer and played great defense. It was his powerful dunks that made him famous, though. Jordan dunked the ball with

Michael Jordan goes up for a reverse layup against the New York Knicks.

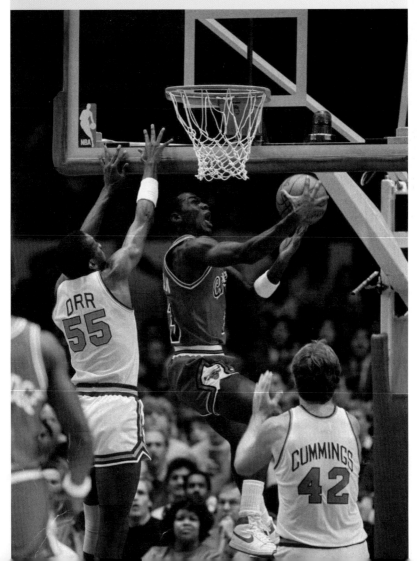

a style and grace that electrified fans. His amazing jump-ing ability soon earned him the nickname "Air Jordan."

Jordan entered the NBA record books that season by becoming the first rookie to lead his team in scoring, **as-sists, rebounds,** and **steals.** His outstanding play earned him the NBA Rookie of the Year title. Jordan reached his goal of leading the Bulls into the play-offs, but they were beaten in the first round.

The Jordan Rules

In the third game of Jordan's second season, he broke a bone in his left foot. It was the first serious injury of his basketball career. Initially the Bulls thought he would re-turn by the middle of the season, but the injury lingered. Jordan finally returned just in time for the 1986 play-offs to face Larry Bird and the Boston Celtics. The Celtics swept the Bulls in three games, but not before Jordan made history. In Game 2 he scored a play-off record sixty-three points. He was already well known at the time, but the game was on national television and his popularity skyrocketed.

The next season, Jordan averaged more than thirty-seven points a game to lead the league in scoring. It was his first NBA scoring title. Bulls fans came to Chicago Stadium to see their high-scoring superstar in record numbers. The year before Jordan's arrival, average atten-dance at the stadium was 6,365. By 1988 all 17,794 seats were filled. Fans around the league also loved watching Jordan perform. Wherever the Bulls played, the stadiums were always sold out.

Jordan passes the ball off in midair. His amazing ability to stay airborne earned him the nickname "Air Jordan."

Jordan won the scoring title again in 1987–1988 and 1988–1989, and both years the Bulls met the Detroit Pistons in the play-offs. The Pistons were nicknamed the "Bad Boys of the NBA" because of their aggressive play. When Jordan drove to the basket, the Detroit defenders swarmed around him and often knocked him to the floor. They called the strategy "The Jordan Rules," and it frustrated him. "The Jordan Rules were a set of defensive principles the Pistons applied to stop me," he said. "As far as I could tell the plan involved running as many guys as possible at me whenever I touched the ball and then hitting me as hard as possible every time I took a shot."[2] The strategy worked because Detroit held Jordan below his season average as they knocked the Bulls out of the play-offs both years.

CHAPTER
THREE

Air Jordan

The Bulls' play-off losses to the Pistons did not dampen Jordan's immense popularity. When he shaved his head in the late 1980s, he became one of the most recognizable sports figures in the world. Advertisers loved his clean image on and off the court. He was featured in television commercials for McDonald's, Coca-Cola, and Gatorade. But the commercials for Nike's Air Jordan shoes marked a high point in his celebrity. The popular commercials showed Jordan beating actor and movie director Spike Lee in a game of one-on-one.

Jordan was most popular among children. Kids around the world idolized him and wore his fashionable Air Jordan shoes. They also bought his Bulls jersey and practiced his moves on neighborhood courts. Jordan

Michael and his mother, Deloris, meet with students during a gathering of the Michael Jordan Foundation in North Carolina in 1996.

showed that children were equally important to him by lending his name to several youth charities. He supported Chicago's Head Start program and the Special Olympics. His love of children went well beyond the "Windy City." He established a charity called the Michael Jordan Foundation to benefit less fortunate children around the world.

Between basketball and his many off court commitments, Jordan had little time for his personal life. That changed in 1989 when he settled down and married Juanita Vanoy. They later had three children: Jasmine, Jeffrey, and Marcus. Jordan discussed how his family provided a focus outside of basketball. "Before I got married and had my family, the public and media got ninety-five percent of my time. Now it's reversed. They help me through tough situations. When I don't have too many people to talk to, I can always talk to my family."[3]

Past the Pistons

Jordan's personal life was more complete, but professionally he wanted more. After five years in the NBA he still had not won a championship. Experts agreed he was the best player in basketball, but they criticized him for shooting the ball too much. They said Chicago would never win a title with him leading the league in scoring. Jordan badly wanted to prove these people wrong.

In 1989 the Bulls hired Phil Jackson as coach, and he immediately installed a team-oriented offense. This meant all five players on the court had a chance to score. It was a dramatic change from the offense that had centered around Jordan the first five years of his career. He

Michael and his wife and children at the Bulls' home opener in 1993. He was retired from basketball at the time.

fought the new system at first, especially when his scoring went down. But he slowly began to accept the offense when the team began to win consistently under Jackson.

The new offense led to the improved play of Jordan's teammate, Scottie Pippen. Pippen, who played in Jor-

Weakened by flu symptoms, Michael Jordan collapses into the arms of teammate Scottie Pippen.

dan's shadow for several years, became an all-star. The teammates played extremely well together on offense and became one of the league's best scoring duos. They also played tight defense, often stealing the ball or forcing opponents to make mistakes. Their outstanding play led the team to fifty-five wins and another play-off appearance. But for the second straight year, the Pistons beat the Bulls in the Eastern Conference Finals, ending Jordan's dream of playing in his first NBA championship.

Although Pippen had become an important part of the team, Jordan was still the leader. In the 1990–1991 season he again led the league in scoring as the Bulls improved to win sixty-one games. After losing to the Pistons in the play-offs three years in a row, the Bulls finally gained revenge by sweeping them in four games.

Jordan was excited at the chance to play the Los Angeles Lakers in his first NBA Finals. He was matched up against one of the league's best players, Magic Johnson. But Jordan quickly showed he was the dominant player by outscoring the Lakers star by nearly a two-to-one margin. The games were close, but in the end the Bulls beat the Lakers four games to two, and Jordan was named series MVP. This award is given to the player who helps his team the most during the course of a series. With the struggle to win a championship finally over, he hugged the trophy and cried tears of joy.

"Three-Peat"

After winning his first NBA title Jordan was even more in the spotlight. A controversial book called *The Jordan*

Jordan's Chicago Bulls
Regular Season Statistics

Year	Games	Field Goal %	Free Throw %	Reb	Ast	Steals	Points
84–85	82	.515	.843	534	481	196	2313
85–86	18	.457	.840	64	53	37	408
86–87	82	.482	.857	430	377	236	3041
87–88	82	.535	.841	449	485	259	2868
88–89	81	.538	.850	652	650	234	2633
89–90	82	.526	.848	565	519	227	2753
90–91	82	.539	.851	492	453	223	2580
91–92	80	.519	.832	511	489	182	2404
92–93	78	.495	.837	522	428	221	2541
93–94		Did	Not	Play			
94–95	17	.411	.801	117	90	30	457
95–96	82	.495	.834	543	352	180	2491
96–97	82	.486	.833	482	353	140	2427

Michael Jordan's Regular Season Facts

1986–1993; 1995–1998	All NBA First Team
1987–1993	All Defense First Team
1987–1988; 1990–1992; 1995–1998	NBA MVP
1986 – 1993; 1995 – 1997	Scoring Champion
1987 – 1988	Defensive Player of the Year

Source: www.NBA.com

Rules claimed that he lost large amounts of money gambling. He later admitted to placing bets with friends on the golf course. The league took the matter seriously and questioned Jordan, but they cleared him of any violations. Still, he was not happy that his image had been tarnished. "The complexity of my life has changed," he said, referring to the negative publicity. "I worked for so many years to get to a point where I'd like to think that I'm one of the best [basketball players]. And now everything—every move, every shot—is in the spotlight. . . . I'm a target now."[4]

Unwelcome Headlines

Next season, Jordan lost his temper during a game and bumped a referee. The league fined and suspended him for one game. It was the first time he had ever gotten that angry on the court, and the incident made the headlines. Basketball fans were stunned to see Jordan had a temper.

Jordan put the controversy behind him, and the Bulls had their best season ever. They finished with sixty-seven wins and advanced to the NBA Finals for the second straight year. Jordan and the Bulls proved to be too strong for their opponent, the Portland Trailblazers. While averaging more than thirty-five points in the series, Jordan led Chicago past Portland four games to two.

Following the Bulls' second championship, Jordan played in the 1992 Summer Olympics in Barcelona, Spain. It was the first time professional players were allowed to compete in the Games. The U.S. team, nicknamed the "Dream Team," was a collection of the NBA's greatest players, and Jordan was the team's brightest star. In a repeat of the 1984 Olympics, Jordan led the U.S. team in scoring as they went undefeated to earn the gold medal.

Once the 1992–1993 NBA season started, Jordan and others raised the possibility of a Bulls "three-peat" (three straight titles). But the Bulls began to show signs they were no longer the league's best team. They failed to reach the sixty-win mark for the first time in three seasons. In the play-offs the team was often on the brink of losing, only to have Jordan sink a key shot or make a crucial steal to secure a win.

Chicago made it to the Finals for the third straight year and faced the Phoenix Suns. Jordan once again outplayed the competition and averaged a play-off record of forty-one points for the series. After winning four games to two, Jordan and the Bulls celebrated their "three-peat."

Back to Baseball

After the Bulls' third title, Jordan felt he had accomplished all that he could in the sport and was growing tired of the grueling NBA lifestyle. He was seriously considering retirement. Then, during the summer of 1993, Jordan suffered a tragic loss. His father, James Jordan, was murdered in his car during an attempted robbery. Michael was devastated. He later reflected on life without his father and best friend. "I no longer had the support and guidance of my father to fall back on. It was my time to become more mature in my approach to life.

Jordan's Chicago Bulls Playoff Statistics

Year	Games	Field Goal %	Free Throw %	Reb	Ast	Steals	Points
84–85	4	.436	.828	23	481	317	117
85–86	3	.505	.872	19	53	37	131
86–87	3	.417	.897	21	377	18	107
87–88	10	.530	.868	71	485	47	363
88–89	17	.510	.799	119	650	130	591
89–90	16	.514	.836	115	519	109	587
90–91	17	.524	.845	108	453	142	529
91–92	22	.499	.857	137	489	127	759
92–93	19	.475	.805	128	428	114	666
93–94		*Did*	*Not*	*Play*			
94–95	10	.484	.810	65	90	45	315
95–96	18	.459	.818	89	352	74	552
96–97	19	.456	.831	150	353	91	590

Michael Jordan's Playoff Facts

1990–1993; 1995–1998	NBA Finals MVP
1998	All-Star game MVP
1998	Member of the *NBA at 50* team
1986–1993; 1995–1997	Scoring Champion

Source: www.NBA.com

Everything I had done to that point, from basketball to business, I passed by my parents. . . . When he died, I realized I had to start making those decisions independent of everyone else. . . . The responsibility was mine alone."[5]

Already leaning toward retirement before his father's death, Jordan announced his decision to leave basketball on October 6, 1993. The sporting world was shocked and saddened to see the league's brightest star retire. He was thirty years old.

Jordan did not stay retired long. He began a professional baseball career by signing a contract with the Chicago White Sox. He had last played baseball as a senior in high school, so he was not yet ready to play in the major leagues. The White Sox sent him to their Double-A team in Birmingham, Alabama, where fans flocked to see him play. He struggled at the beginning and his **batting average** was just above .200. But when he hit .259 over the last month of the 1993 season, he showed he could compete in the sport. He returned for the 1994 season and was one of only six players to have fifty runs batted in and thirty stolen bases. Then Major League Baseball went on strike. Unsure of when the season would resume, he decided to end his baseball career.

The Comeback

Playing baseball had given Jordan a chance to escape from the basketball spotlight. But after eighteen months away from the game he loved, he felt refreshed and ready to come back. He secretly practiced with the Bulls for several weeks, then on March 18, 1995, he announced his return when he faxed a two-word statement to the press that read, "I'm back." He was not coming back as number twenty-three, though. That number had been retired when Jordan left the Bulls in 1993. Instead, he wore number forty-five, his brother Larry's high school basketball number and the number Michael wore playing baseball.

In his third game back Jordan scored fifty-five points against the New York Knicks, and it looked as if he had

Jordan in his "second" career with the Bulls as Number 45. He returned to basketball after a brief retirement spent playing baseball.

never retired. But in reality his body was not in condition for basketball, and he started to wear down at the end of the season. He gathered enough energy to lift the Bulls into the play-offs, where they were matched against the Orlando Magic. Jordan made several crucial mistakes that hurt his team. A Magic player stole the ball from him late in one of the games, which led to Orlando's winning basket. He switched back to his old number for good luck, but the Bulls lost the series anyway. Afterward, fans said Jordan's comeback was a mistake, because he was slower and had lost his outstanding jumping ability.

After the bitter loss to Orlando, Jordan vowed to prove his critics wrong and practiced hard to regain his skills that summer. Working around his basketball schedule, he found time to make the movie *Space Jam*. Sharing the screen with Bugs Bunny, Daffy Duck, and other Warner Brothers cartoon characters, the movie mirrored his real-life return to basketball. But fiction proved to be far better than reality. In the movie he came back from baseball to beat a team of alien monsters on the basketball court.

Decade of Dominance

Jordan returned for the 1995–1996 season a quicker, more determined player than ever. He averaged thirty-plus

Michael Jordan costarred with Warner Brothers cartoon characters in the movie Space Jam.

points a game as the Bulls beat opponents with ease. At one point they won eighteen games in a row. They finished the season with an NBA record seventy-two wins.

Jordan and the Bulls proved to be equally as hard to beat in the play-offs. They advanced to the Finals, where

Exhausted and relieved, Jordan hoists the 1996 championship trophy in the air.

they defeated the Seattle Supersonics in six games. Afterward, he showed another emotional side of himself. The game was played on Father's Day, and memories of his dad came flooding back. In a touching scene, he clutched the game ball while laying facedown on the locker room floor and sobbed uncontrollably.

A Heroic Performance

After the Bulls' fourth championship Jordan was determined to win his fifth the next season. For the second straight year the Bulls finished the regular season with the NBA's best record. They returned to the championship, where they faced the Utah Jazz. It looked as if the Bulls might finally lose in the Finals when, with the series tied at two games apiece, Jordan was hit with a severe stomach virus. He played in Game 5 and gave a heroic performance. Battling through severe **nausea**, he made several clutch shots, then scored the winning basket with twenty-five seconds remaining. The Bulls beat the Jazz in the next game to win their fifth championship.

When the 1997–1998 season started, the press began to write that Jordan was going to retire at the end of the year. He would not confirm the reports, but Coach Phil Jackson's contract ended that year and Jordan suggested to reporters he would not play for another coach. Even with the rumor surrounding the team much of the season, Jordan led the Bulls back to the Finals to face the Utah Jazz. Chicago led the series three games to two but were behind by one point late in Game 6. With the clock ticking down, Jordan stole the ball. Then, with six seconds remaining, he scored the game-winning shot. The Utah fans stood in stunned silence as Jordan and his teammates celebrated.

Family Man

Bulls fans around the world also celebrated the team's sixth championship, but there was less enthusiasm than in years past. The difference was that they knew Jordan had probably played his final game in Chicago. As expected, before the start of the 1998–1999 season, the Bulls hired a coach to replace Jackson. Jordan considered playing for the New York Knicks, but in the end, he walked away from the game. He gave his reasons at a press conference: "I've accomplished everything I could as an individual, and right now I don't have the mental challenges that I have had in the past to proceed as a basketball player. . . . This is a perfect time for me to walk away from the game."[6]

In his retirement he spent most of his time with his family. He often got the children ready in the morning and drove them to and from school. He was devoted to them, much like his father was to him when he was growing up in North Carolina. But even in retirement Jordan found himself in the national spotlight. In 1999 he received perhaps the greatest award ever given to an athlete. The cable sports channel ESPN counted down the fifty greatest athletes of the twentieth century. In a list that included golf's Jack Nicklaus, boxing's Muhammad Ali, and baseball's Babe Ruth, Jordan was at the top. It was a fitting end to his amazing career with the Bulls.

Wizard on the Court

Although Jordan was happy in retirement, he was lured back to the NBA in 2000—not as a player, but as president of basketball operations for the Washington Wizards. He also bought a share of the team to become a part owner. He spent time in Washington, D.C., working for the team and returned home to Chicago to see his family at every opportunity. In 2001 Jordan surprised the sports world when he announced his return to the game as a player for the Wizards, one of the worst teams in basketball the previous season.

At age thirty-eight, Jordan was a step slower, but he made up for it with his great intelligence and vision on the court. Instead of trying to beat defenders to the hoop for a dunk, he set up scoring opportunities for teammates by passing the ball more. He still led the Wizards in scoring, but it was nearly eight points below his career average. Where he helped the most, though, was in providing leadership to the young team. Washington was

Jordan announces his retirement from basketball at a press conference in 1999.

26-21 when the NBA paused for the All-Star game. It was the team's best record at that point in the season in twenty-three years.

When the season resumed, Jordan developed a sore knee. Eventually the knee required surgery, and he missed

Jordan in his "third" NBA career with the Washington Wizards again wore Number 23, the number retired by the Chicago Bulls after his first retirement in 1993.

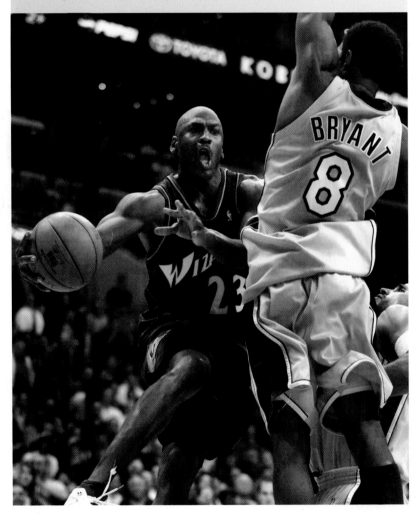

almost an entire month. When he returned the knee still bothered him, so he decided to sit out the rest of the season. The Wizards' chances of making the play-offs ended soon after they lost Jordan. It was the first time in his career his team missed the play-offs.

To some people Jordan damaged his reputation when he came out of retirement a slower, lower-scoring player in 2001. But to others he strengthened his image as champion by giving

Michael Jordan shows frustration with the play of his Washington teammates in his first game as a Wizard in 2001.

the Wizards a chance to win. Whatever the future holds for Jordan, basketball experts claim the world will never see another player with his ability or will to win, but he disagrees. "Somewhere there is a little kid working to enhance what [I've] done. It may take awhile, but someone will come along who approaches the game the way I did. . . . Maybe he will take off from the free-throw line and do a 360 in midair. . . . Unless they change the height of the basket or otherwise alter the dimensions of the game, there will be a player much greater than me."[7]

Notes

Chapter Two: A Rising Star
1. Quoted in CBS FOX Video Sports, "Michael Jordan: Air Time," 1993.
2. Quoted in Michael Jordan, *For the Love of the Game*. New York: Crown, 1998, p. 11.

Chapter Three: Air Jordan
3. Quoted in CBS FOX Video Sports, "Michael Jordan."
4. Quoted in CBS FOX Video Sports, "Michael Jordan."
5. Quoted in Jordan, *For the Love of the Game*, p. 106.

Chapter Four: The Comeback
6. Quoted in *Online NewsHour*, "Online Focus: King of the Court," January 13, 1999. www.PBS.org.
7. Quoted in Jordan, *For the Love of the Game*, p. 155.

Glossary

airborne: In the air, or aloft.

All-American: An award given to the best college athletes in the nation.

assist: A pass that leads directly to a teammate scoring a basket.

batting average: The average number of times a batter gets a base hit compared to the number of at bats; base hits divided by at bats (example: 3 hits in 10 at bats equals .300 batting average).

nausea: Sickness usually accompanied by vomiting or lightheadedness.

rebound: Occurs when a player gains possession of the ball after a missed shot.

steal: The act of taking away the ball from a player on the opposing team.

For Further Exploration

Books

Nathan Aaseng, *Sports Great: Michael Jordan*. Springfield, NJ: Enslow, 1997. Highlights the life and career of the NBA's greatest player.

Bob Condor, *Michael Jordan's 50 Greatest Games*. Secaucus, NJ: Citadel, 1998. Ranks Jordan's fifty greatest games, complete with game stories and statistics.

Bill Gutman, *Teammates: Michael Jordan & Scottie Pippen*. Brookfield, CT: Millbrook, 1998. Focuses on the special on-court relationship between Jordan and Pippen.

Michael Jordan, *For the Love of the Game*. New York: Crown, 1998. Jordan's only autobiography to date, it examines his rise as a star and features personal stories about his relationships with teammates and coaches.

Thomas R. Raber, *Michael Jordan: Basketball Skywalker*, Minneapolis: Lerner, 1997. Gives a thorough account of Jordan's rise from his days as a high school star to the greatest player in the game.

Internet Source
ESPN.com, Michael Jordan (http://sports.espn.go.com).
Includes a player profile, up-to-date statistics, game logs,
and other miscellaneous statistics.

Websites
Michael Jordan Official Website (http://jordan.
sportsline.com). Includes a player biography, statistics,
merchandise, a Jordan trivia challenge, and more.

Michael Jordan Player Info (www.nba.com). An excel-
lent resource for team news, in-depth statistics, and career highlights.

Index

About the Author

Raymond H. Miller is the author of more than fifty non-fiction books for children. He has written on a range of topics from sports trivia to poisonous animals. He enjoys playing sports and spending time outdoors with his wife and daughter.